Learn how to earn **double-digit** returns
trading the financial
10 minutes or less

HOW TO *Build*
Wealth

BILL POULOS
Profits Run

How To Build Wealth

To my wife, Karen, and my children, Greg, Rob, & Mike, whose love and understanding has made all of this possible.

Also, to my team at Profits Run. Your hard work and dedication have helped thousands of people from all walks of life become better traders.

Finally, to my students. You are the reason Greg and I started Profits Run in 2001. You've made me a better trader myself and you're the reason we're able to do what we do today. Thank you.

Table of Contents

Foreword

One night in the year 2000 I was over at my parents' house having dinner. My dad, Bill, was set to retire 12 years early from a 36 year career at General Motors the following year, and the software development company that I worked for at the time was going to be closing its sole Michigan office. So both of us were going to be out of a job.

My dad was able to retire early in part because of his experience trading the markets, which is his true passion. I have many childhood memories of him coming home from work, grabbing a quick bite to eat with the family, and then disappearing for hours in his home office. I'd poke my head in occasionally and see him staring through a magnifying glass at piles of printed charts, which were delivered daily to our house. He was constantly drawing lines on those charts with a mechanical pencil and a straightedge, and he always had a pad of graph paper on his desk filled with data from his latest trading experiment. This was way before computers, so he did all his analysis using nothing more than those printed charts and a calculator. He's definitely always been somewhat of a *trading nerd*.

We were never rich when I was growing up. We were just an average middle class family, and my dad's family never had a lot of money, so he basically is the textbook definition of a self-made man. He went to school, got good grades, stayed out of trouble, got a good job, and just worked really, really hard. And in his spare time he learned the secrets of what it takes to build wealth trading the markets.

So when we were sitting around the dinner table that night in 2000 we were discussing what we were going to do when I said to him, "Hey, why don't we teach people what you've learned about the markets?"

And that's when we decided to start our financial education company, Profits Run. We named it after the old trading maxim, "Cut your losses and let your profits run". We spent a year developing our first product and officially launched in 2001. We literally started at the kitchen table and now, years later, we have a modest office with a full time staff of professional traders and coaches.

I always encouraged my dad to write a book to introduce people to his trading philosophy. So I'm happy that he finally did it.

The information you're about to read in the following pages is somewhat contrarian to how the general public thinks money is made in the markets. But as you probably know, most people do not know how to make money in the markets. And as you're about to find out, building true wealth over time trading the markets is indeed possible, and it's easier than you probably think.

Figure 1 - Bill & Greg Poulos, 2012

It's been a lot of fun helping my dad build our business. At last count we've helped over 40,000 regular people from all around the world become better traders, and I hope you pick up some good techniques from this book that will help you become a better trader yourself.

Greg Poulos

Introduction

Hi, my name is Bill Poulos. I started trading the markets back in 1974 when I was working at General Motors. I had a great wife and two young sons and I wanted the best for my family. I knew that working hard at GM could only provide a certain level of income, so I spent every spare minute learning how to trade. Little did I know at the time that I was beginning a lifelong odyssey that would eventually touch the lives of tens of thousands of people.

I was born and raised in Detroit, Michigan, to a lower middle class family, so I had to work hard to get where I am at today. At one point I was the youngest Eagle Scout in the Detroit area. I earned a Bachelor of Industrial Engineering degree at General Motors Institute, and then went on to get my MBA in finance from the University of Michigan.

Hard work is a quality my father instilled in me, and while I had to work hard to discover the trading principles you're going to learn in this book, you're luckier than I was. That's because if you apply what you learn here, you won't have to work nearly as hard as I did to have a good chance at building wealth in the markets.

I made every mistake you can make in trading. I tried, tested, and bought just about every book and system I could get my hands on, and I traveled to as many seminars as possible. I developed dozens of my own systems but quickly became bored and impatient when they experienced a few losing trades. I, like so many other young and inexperienced beginners before me, was searching for the illusive *Holy Grail* of trading. I was young and naïve and thought without a doubt that I could "crack the code" and discover the system that everyone has been looking for since the dawn of the markets.

Figure 2 - Around the time I started trading in 1974

I'll admit it, I was stubborn for many years, but one day I *finally got it*. I finally "cracked the code". After spending thousands and thousands of dollars on systems, and an equal number of hours locked away in my home office, I finally learned that the *Holy Grail* of trading just doesn't exist. But the biggest surprise I learned was that you don't need the *Holy Grail* of trading in order to have the potential to build lifelong wealth in the markets. And that's good news!

I learned the hard way that while it is possible to profit from the markets trading correctly, it is a near certainty that you will lose money trading incorrectly.

Then one day, my son, Greg, asked if I wanted to start a business with him teaching others what took me so long to learn. I was retiring, but I had no intention of sitting around and golfing all day. So I was looking for something to do anyway, and Greg's offer was too irresistible to pass up.

But I think what really inspired me to start helping others was that I was so tired watching all the shameless hucksters on the Internet and cable TV hype their baseless opinions, useless systems, and empty promises. So I wanted to help set the record straight and help the "regular guy" avoid all that nonsense. And then *something magical happened.*

I found the more I shared with others about what I knew about trading, the more I learned! You've heard it said before, and I can attest to the fact that it's true: the more you teach others about what you know, the better you understand what you know. As I interacted with more and more people who used my trading methods, I began to make an already good method even better.

And now years later, I've developed some core trading concepts that are common to every trading method I teach. These concepts are really the culmination of my life's work at trading the markets. This is the kind of information that I want to pass on to my family, and that I hope my children pass on to their children. This has the real potential to create *generational wealth*. And if you've traded before, I'm willing to bet that the concepts in this book are probably dramatically different than anything you've already seen or tried.

It's also important to understand that the information in this book goes against how most people think money is made in the markets. It is even doubtful that your financial advisor or broker knows about the principles I'm going to reveal here. But, as you probably know, most people lose in the markets, and your financial advisor or broker make money regardless of how your portfolio performs.

So, sit back and relax. Close the door. Turn off your phone and your computer. Get comfortable, and dive in.

I can't promise that this book will make you rich (nobody can promise that), but I can promise you that after you read it you'll understand the core principles that you need to have the potential to build lifelong wealth in the markets by trading 10 minutes per day or less.

Good Trading,

Bill Poulos

p.s. Make sure you visit **www.BuildWealthBonus.com** where you'll find my step-by-step trading course along with extra bonus training materials, valued at $497, yours free for reading this book.

Chapter 1

What 'They' Don't Want You To Know

There's something that the richest of the rich, *the super elite*, don't want you to know. If you've struggled to make money and build wealth in the past, *it's not your fault.* Whether through intentional misinformation or just plain ignorance, you've been lied to most of your life by the "powers that be" about how to make money in the markets.

And if you think that sounds like some crazy conspiracy theory mumbo-jumbo, you're kidding yourself, because the evidence has been in plain sight. It will all be clear by the end of this book, but for now just recognize that there are indeed two different sets of rules: one for the ultra wealthy, and one for the rest of us.

What have we all been taught in one way or another since we were kids? That it takes hard work to get ahead, to succeed, and to get rich. As I explained in the introduction, I was taught this, too. And while hard work got me a great corporate career and helped me live comfortably as part of the upper middle class, it never helped me go past that, into the realm of the wealthy.

How To Build Wealth

Don't get me wrong, there's nothing bad about hard work. But you need more than hard work to truly build wealth. You need to work *differently* than everybody else. You to need to work *smarter*. You need to tap into *the rules that the ultra rich play by*.

The fact that you're even reading a book about wealth-building says a lot about you and your character. It shows me that you're different than most people and that you feel like you have what it takes to really step up and provide for yourself and your family like you know you and they deserve.

I have to confess that it took me a long time to see through the misdirection that constantly gets fed to us *regular people* by the big financial power players. Had I caught on sooner, I could've provided more to my family, more quickly. But now that I clearly see what's going on, I'm satisfied in knowing that my children, and *their* children will have a huge advantage as they go forward in the world.

So while this is a book about trading the financial markets to have the potential to build wealth, it's ultimately about way more than that. It's about realizing that there is *specialized knowledge* that the wealthy use to their advantage every day that often is the complete opposite of how most people are taught to do things.

How To Build Wealth

And that's exactly what you're going to learn in this book: specialized knowledge that the wealthy use to their advantage to pull as much profit potential as possible out of the markets, as safely as possible, and with as little work as possible.

But I must caution you about a strange phenomenon that has to do with human nature. As you learn about the concepts, strategies, and tactics I'm going to reveal in this book, you're going to be tempted to tell your family and friends about them. And when you actually implement what you learn and start to see results, you might be tempted to even tell complete strangers about what you're experiencing.

While it's understandable that you may feel this way, be prepared for them to be skeptical. Be prepared for them to shut you down. And be prepared for them to flat-out argue with you that you're wrong.

There's a well-known concept called "crab mentality", or "crabs in the bucket", that may be best summed up by the phrase, "if I can't have it, neither can you." It goes like this. If there's a pot full of crabs, individually they could easily escape the pot. But what they do instead is grab at any crab trying to escape, which ensures that they'll all remain trapped in the pot.

That's kind of what tends to happen when you try to push through the "norm" that your family or social group is comfortable with. They're just trying to protect you because they haven't learned yet what you have come to know as the truth.

So, by all means share what you learn. Just be prepared for this natural resistance and give people time to accept your newfound enthusiasm and knowledge.

Chapter 2

Develop A Wealth Mindset

Before I dive into the specifics around how to build wealth in the markets, it's necessary to first establish what is perhaps the most important quality you must possess to accomplish that goal.

I'm talking about having a realistic wealth mindset. And no, I don't mean mindset as in positive thinking or the power of manifestation, although I believe those are good things, too.

What I mean is more a practical, pragmatic understanding of how wealthy individuals think, especially compared to those who are not wealthy.

And despite what the media would have you believe, there's more opportunity than ever right now in the markets.

But I think the reason most people don't know that is because of this great quote from Thomas Edison.

He said, *"Opportunity is missed by most people because it is dressed in overalls and looks like work."*

In other words, most people completely miss out on opportunity because they're afraid it's going to be too much work.

And when it comes to trading the markets, I believe that one of the main reasons over 90% of regular people lose money is because they over-complicate their approach to trading and investing and give up because it's just too much work.

But you know what?

Over-complicating trading is easy to do. After all, there's a ton of conflicting information online, in books, at seminars, and on TV. And, many of the so-called "gurus" are teaching trading strategies that are, quite frankly, needlessly complicated.

And if there's one thing I've learned from trading the markets since 1974, it's that if a trading strategy is too complicated, you won't follow it properly, which will lead to mistakes, which ultimately leads to losing trades.

It's one of the key trading secrets you were never taught that some of the world's most successful traders already discovered.

And that secret is that "simple is better".

I don't know about others, but I first stumbled upon this concept when I found this profound quote by Albert Einstein.

He said, *"Everything should be made as simple as possible, but not simpler."*

And that quote is the basis for not only this book, but for everything I do and teach at Profits Run.

One of the traits that wealthy people possess is that they tend to never over-complicate things. They keep it simple. In fact, many successful business owners have said that they can fit their entire business plan on the back of a napkin, and that's one of the keys to their success.

Here's another little secret of amassing true wealth, whether it's trading, real estate investing, or even starting your own business.

It all has to do with the timeframe that you *think in*, and I'm not talking about the timeframe of a stock chart. Here's what I mean.

Amateurs expect to strike it rich almost immediately and they get frustrated if everything doesn't go their way. For example, in trading, amateurs expect to win every trade, or they expect to make money every week. And if their expectations aren't met, they mistakenly conclude that their approach is invalid and they give up and go on the hunt for another "get rich quick" scheme.

This is why amateurs remain poor, because *the poor think in weeks*.

January

S	M	T	W	T	F	S
		1	2	3	4	5
6	7	8	9	10	11	12
13	14	15	16	17	18	19
20	21	22	23	24	25	26
27	28	29	30	31		

Figure 3 - The poor think in weeks

The middle class, on the other hand, think in months. Their major financial concerns tend to be their monthly bills, like their home mortgage, car payment, credit card payments, and so on.

January

S	M	T	W	T	F	S
		1	2	3	4	5
6	7	8	9	10	11	12
13	14	15	16	17	18	19
20	21	22	23	24	25	26
27	28	29	30	31		

February

S	M	T	W	T	F	S
					1	2
3	4	5	6	7	8	9
10	11	12	13	14	15	16
17	18	19	20	21	22	23
24	25	26	27	28		

March

S	M	T	W	T	F	S
					1	2
3	4	5	6	7	8	9
10	11	12	13	14	15	16
17	18	19	20	21	22	23
24	25	26	27	28	29	30
31						

April

S	M	T	W	T	F	S
		1	2	3	4	5	6
7	8	9	10	11	12	13
14	15	16	17	18	19	20
21	22	23	24	25	26	27
28	29	30				

May

S	M	T	W	T	F	S
			1	2	3	4
5	6	7	8	9	10	11
12	13	14	15	16	17	18
19	20	21	22	23	24	25
26	27	28	29	30	31	

June

S	M	T	W	T	F	S
						1
2	3	4	5	6	7	8
9	10	11	12	13	14	15
16	17	18	19	20	21	22
23	24	25	26	27	28	29
30						

July

S	M	T	W	T	F	S
	1	2	3	4	5	6
7	8	9	10	11	12	13
14	15	16	17	18	19	20
21	22	23	24	25	26	27
28	29	30	31			

August

S	M	T	W	T	F	S
				1	2	3
4	5	6	7	8	9	10
11	12	13	14	15	16	17
18	19	20	21	22	23	24
25	26	27	28	29	30	31

September

S	M	T	W	T	F	S
1	2	3	4	5	6	7
8	9	10	11	12	13	14
15	16	17	18	19	20	21
22	23	24	25	26	27	28
29	30					

October

S	M	T	W	T	F	S
		1	2	3	4	5
6	7	8	9	10	11	12
13	14	15	16	17	18	19
20	21	22	23	24	25	26
27	28	29	30	31		

November

S	M	T	W	T	F	S
					1	2
3	4	5	6	7	8	9
10	11	12	13	14	15	16
17	18	19	20	21	22	23
24	25	26	27	28	29	30

December

S	M	T	W	T	F	S
1	2	3	4	5	6	7
8	9	10	11	12	13	14
15	16	17	18	19	20	21
22	23	24	25	26	27	28
29	30	31				

Figure 4 - The middle class think in months

The rich think in years. They think more about investments, financial education, building businesses, and multiple streams of income.

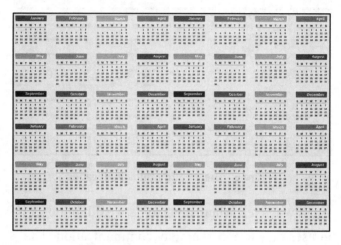

Figure 5 - The rich think in years

And the wealthy? They think in decades. They think about asset protection, how to minimize their taxes, how to best have their money work for them, how to create and grow charities, and how to establish a legacy for their children and future generations.

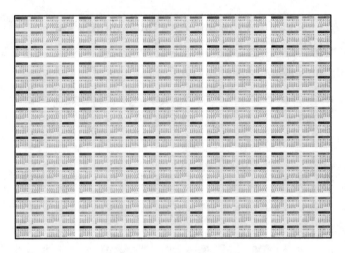

Figure 6 - The wealthy think in decades

I can always tell where a person's wealth mindset is by the phrases they use in everyday communication. The things they say are telltale signs of the timeframe in which they think.

Another trait that wealthy people possess is that they take responsibility for their own successes and failures. They never blame others.

No matter what problems they are born with or have attracted throughout life, they never use those problems as an excuse for failure.

Instead, they take on an attitude of *failing fast*, because they understand that with each failure comes more experience and more knowledge. Thus, the faster they can fail, the quicker they can succeed.

How To Build Wealth

Wealthy people constantly invest in bettering themselves by reading books, attending seminars, and working with coaches. In fact, if you walk into the home of a wealthy person, you'll probably find a large collection of books somewhere, if not an entire home library.

Here's an interesting side note. As you learn more and more about any particular subject, the amount of new information you can learn becomes smaller and smaller. So the first time you read a book on a subject, 90% of what you read may be brand new. By the time you read a tenth book on the same subject, maybe only 10% of what you read is new to you. Well, wealthy people understand this, and when they read books or attend seminars they're just looking for one more useful tidbit or nugget of information. They know that 90% will be a repeat of what they already have learned. And they also know that many times just one more idea is all it takes to push them forward exponentially.

Finally, wealthy people also have an abundance mentality. They tend to be some of the most generous people on the planet, openly sharing their time, knowledge, and money with others, not in the expectation of getting something back, but for the sake of paying it forward.

Yes, there are wealthy people who are selfish and greedy and who take advantage of others, but these are few and far between. I've never met any wealthy people like that, but I've met plenty of poor people who act that way.

So, as you go forward building wealth, you'll get there much more quickly and it will be much easier if you adopt the traits that wealthy people possess.

Don't forget to visit **www.BuildWealthBonus.com** to claim your free bonus wealth building training materials.

Chapter 3

Why You Need To Be Trading

We are living in a pretty scary world right now, at least economically speaking. You may already have a nice portfolio that you are trying to safeguard. Or, if you're like most people, you're struggling to just "stay afloat" and pay the monthly bills, not to mention figuring out how you're going to fund your retirement.

That's why you need to take action and change the way you handle your finances right now; because if you don't change, the forces in the economy have a very real chance of destroying your family's financial future.

And I'm not talking about 20 or 30 years from now. I'm talking in the coming months and years.

Just look at the facts:

- 1 out of 4 Americans are under-employed or unemployed (28%), according to a recent Gallup Poll...

- 69% of these people are more stressed than ever...

- Of those that *are* employed, job satisfaction has dropped over 16% in just 15 years, according to the Conference Board...

- We are living longer and life expectancy continues to grow. There are over 44 million people that are over the age of 65; up from 3.1 million in 1900...

- Most experts believe the average person will need between 70% and 80% of their income to live comfortably...

- ...yet, very few people are properly planning their financial future.

But perhaps the biggest problem facing most regular people today who want to grow their portfolio consistently so that they have a chance to retire relatively young is that the tried and true "buy & hold" approach to investing simply doesn't work anymore. It's a relic of the 20th Century. And not only does it not work anymore, but there's a strong argument to be made that it will never work again.

If you're unfamiliar with the term "buy & hold", let's do a quick review. It's an investment strategy based on the belief that the market always goes up in the long run. That assumption has been the cornerstone behind pretty much

every so-called financial advisor's diversification strategy
that they peddle to the unsuspecting public.

And for a while, it worked out just fine.

Look at this chart of the S&P500 from 1991 through the
end of 2001.

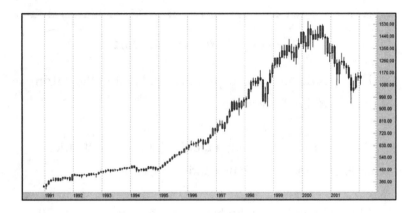

Figure 7 - S&P500 from 1991 - 2001

For the first 9 years of this chart, a buy & hold strategy
was probably a good move. You didn't have to be a genius
to have a good shot at making money in the markets.

But it all started to fall apart around 2001. However,
most investors thought the market would correct and
continue its climb like it did for most of the 90's.

Well, of course, that didn't happen, as you can see in
this S&P500 chart of the subsequent 10 years.

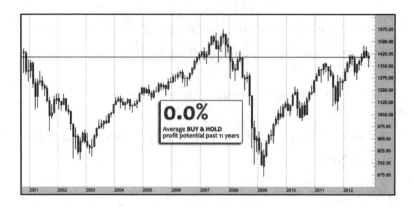

Figure 8 - S&P500 from 2001 - 2012

This decade pretty much put the final nail in the coffin of the buy & hold investing strategy.

Over a period of 11 years the S&P500 was flat, after experiencing many huge ups and downs.

Almost everybody who had open positions in early 2008 went into shock by the end of that year when the market crashed hard.

Of course, there's no way to predict any of these market moves, but the good news is that you don't have to predict anything to be able to have the potential to make a lot of money in a market like this.

Let me show you what I mean.

Here's another chart of the S&P500, this time zoomed in to a 9-month period.

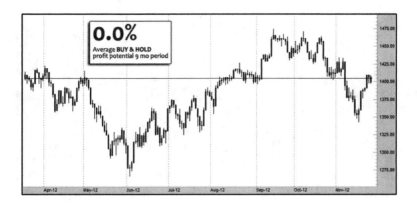

Figure 9 - S&P500, 9-Month Period

A buy & hold investor would have seen their portfolio at breakeven over this period, and that's if they were able to keep their positions open and ride out the storm, which is very tough to do.

What do you tell your spouse when you have to cancel that vacation you were planning on taking because you just took a big loss, and you have no idea how to recover? It's not an easy situation to be in.

Well, if you look at this same 9-month period through the eyes of a trader, this is what you see:

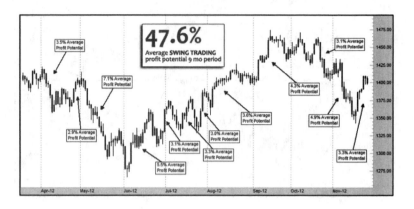

Figure 10 - S&P500 9-Month Period Trading Potential

A whopping 47.6% of profit potential by trading the short-term trends that are literally everywhere on this chart.

Now, just to be clear, this is assuming you're using a good swing trading method, and this is profit *potential*. That doesn't mean you would've made 47.6%, but it does mean that a good method had a good chance at getting a lot of that potential.

However, it *is* a realistic goal to earn double-digit returns every year trading 10 minutes or less per day. Can you earn 99% or more a year? It's not likely, but it could happen. Would you be happy with 20% per year? That's definitely a more realistic goal and almost anyone would be thrilled with results like that.

The bottom line is that there's no way to guarantee the results going forward of any trading method. Even a published record of past trades is no indication that the same kind of performance will hold in the future.

So don't get caught in the trap of just looking at performance results when considering a trading method. The only way for you to know if a method is going to work for you is to try it out for yourself.

The best you can do is to go after short-term trends and maximize your odds of success every time you trade by managing risk first and then having a strategy for pulling as much profit potential out of the market as possible.

That's exactly what short-term traders do, and that's what this book will help you achieve.

And, thankfully, that's all that's really needed to have the potential to build substantial wealth trading the markets in your lifetime.

So, the choice is really yours. There are two different realities, and the question you should be asking yourself is: which one do you choose?

And, you can probably see the urgency around making a decision today versus tomorrow about what to do with your portfolio.

You ultimately need to make a choice:

1. You can gamble on the now obsolete "buy & hold" approach and hope and pray the market goes up and does not drop again by 40% or more.

2. You can take responsibility for your own financial future and learn how to successfully trade the short-term trends that appear again and again if you know where to find them.

I'm assuming you're taking route number two; otherwise you wouldn't be reading this. After all, you're the only one who really cares about your finances. Your broker certainly doesn't. He makes money every time you trade, regardless if you win or lose. Your financial advisor isn't going to help much, either. He has a lot of clients and it's usually not practical to give your portfolio the kind of focus and attention that it deserves. Besides, he's only trying to match the performance of the major market indices, even if they drop 40%. And the government is *definitely* not looking out for your best interests. They're more focused on figuring out how they can take *more* of your income and savings. So, it really comes down to *you*.

But that's good news. Because when you finally choose to take responsibility for your portfolio, you never again have to worry about what the media is reporting. You never again have to worry when the market crashes again (which it *will* do many more times in your lifetime). And, you never again have to worry about what policies or controls the government enacts.

That's because you will know exactly what to do, no matter what happens in the markets. You'll have a step-by-step plan that manages risk first and foremost, and then leaves room for you to capture as much profit potential as possible.

It's just a great way to manage your portfolio, and I can't wait for you to experience it firsthand.

For a deeper analysis of how buy & hold strategies actually performed since 1901, make sure you visit **www.BuildWealthBonus.com**.

Chapter 4

Technical vs. Fundamental Analysis

In order to trade the markets, you need to have a way to analyze them so that you can make good trading decisions. There are basically two broad types of market analysis: *technical analysis* and *fundamental analysis*. The purpose of both is to attempt to determine the most likely future direction of any market, such as a stock or an exchange-traded fund (ETF).

And when you have a good idea of where a market is headed, then you have an edge over other traders because the odds are in your favor of the expected move occurring. It has often been said that if you don't know what your edge is when trading the markets, then you don't have one. And if you don't have an edge and attempt to trade, you're just guessing, or flat-out gambling. So that is why some sort of analysis is required.

There has been a long and lively debate over these two very different types of market analysis ever since the markets came into play. In general, investors with a longer-term outlook on the markets tend to favor fundamental analysis, whereas traders with a shorter-term outlook on the markets tend to favor technical analysis.

If you're a fundamental analyst, then you study macro economic data (both domestic and international) as well as sector, industry and company-specific performance data. On the other hand, if you're a technical analyst, then you believe all economic and company-specific performance data is already baked into the price of the company's stock and therefore you focus exclusively on studying price charts.

If you favor fundamental analysis, before you invest in a company, you have to be prepared to dive deep into an exhausting list of information, such as economic growth rates, Federal Reserve interest rate and money supply policy, unemployment data, non-farm payroll reports, consumer sentiment reports, earnings announcements and forward guidance, dividend yield, earnings growth rates, sales growth rates, competitive threats, political risks, price-earnings ratios, net book value, and so on.

$$\text{Price-Earnings Ratio} = \frac{\text{Market Value per Share}}{\text{Earnings per Share (EPS)}}$$

Figure 11 - Price-earnings ratio formula used in fundamental analysis

It should be obvious from this partial list of fundamental factors that such analysis requires a great deal of rigor and time. Further, in today's world of instant communication and rapidly changing events, fundamental analysis must be done on a timely basis to be relevant.

However, I've found that fundamental analysis really isn't all that useful in helping to determine which way the market is going to move. This is because the markets are driven by fear and greed, plain and simple. So you could spend weeks analyzing a company's fundamental data only to have all your work become meaningless almost overnight, derailed by plain old human psychology. Also, it's a well-known fact that fear and greed can send a bull market far higher and a bear market far lower than fundamental analysis would predict. I'm not saying to completely ignore fundamental analysis, but it's important to recognize its limitations.

If you favor technical analysis, on the other hand, then you tend to look for patterns in historical data that you hope will repeat again in the future. You do this by studying the price charts of a market, where you have at your disposal over 100 technical indicators. These are simply visual elements calculated from the open, close, high, and low prices of each bar and which are overlaid on a chart. Some common technical indicators include moving averages, the average directional index (ADX), the stochastic oscillator, and more.

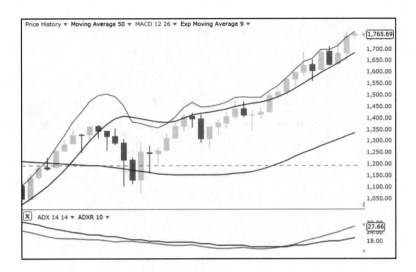

Figure 12 - Typical chart with indicators (FreeStockCharts.com)

If you're a technical analyst then you have it easier than a fundamental analyst because all known fundamental information is immediately reflected in the price of the market you are considering. However, technical analysis can be complicated or it can be simple. It's really up to you as the trader to decide. Beginner traders tend to use far too many technical indicators, which can create "analysis paralysis" and hopeless confusion. In fact, the more indicators that you apply to your analysis, the less likely such analysis will be helpful. But remember Einstein! Simple is indeed better, especially here, because all you really need are a handful of indicators that complement each other and that are simple to interpret.

Now, there is no magic in these technical indicators and they won't lead to the *Holy Grail* of trading. In fact, applying these indicators in commonly understood "textbook" fashion like most traders are taught to do does not generally predict prices any better than throwing a dart. On the other hand, when you apply commonly used indicators in an *uncommon* way, you can indeed get a powerful edge over other traders.

However, there *are* times when fundamental type events should be considered, even if you primarily use technical analysis. One such time is when a major news event is about to occur, regardless if it is company-specific (especially earnings announcements), or when a government economic report is about to be released (especially Federal Reserve announcements and unemployment data). In that case, it is best to *stand aside* and pause trading. Stay out of the market until the event has passed. Some news events will pass with virtually no noticeable effect at all on the markets; however, some events will cause a great deal of volatility in the price action. It can be difficult to tell which events will move the markets and in what direction, and which will not. So it is best to simply stand aside and only re-enter the market afterwards as your trading method dictates.

The bottom line is this. If you apply a good trading method based on technical analysis with discipline, and if you avoid markets in the midst of major economic or company specific announcements, then you have the opportunity to do very, very well trading the markets while having the potential to build wealth throughout your lifetime.

For a free, in-depth guide on the basics of trading, including more details on fundamental and technical analysis, go to **www.BuildWealthBonus.com** to download a copy of *Trading for Beginners*.

Chapter 5

Trading Vehicles

It may come as a surprise to you that there really isn't one perfect trading vehicle, or market, that can build wealth faster than another. It really comes down to personal preference. Everybody is different. Some people like trading stocks, while others prefer to trade exchange-traded funds (ETFs).

Let's take a look at the different types of trading vehicles, how they work, and the benefits and risks of each type.

Stocks – A stock is a security issued by a corporation that represents a proportionate percentage of ownership rights in the assets of the corporation less corporate liabilities and obligations and of course, a proportionate share of profits or losses. Shares of stock are reflected in stock certificates. Each share represents a standard unit of ownership in a corporation. A stockholder is a real owner of a corporation's property, which is held in the name of the corporation for the benefit of all its stockholders. Stocks differ from other securities such as notes and bonds, which are corporate obligations that do not represent an ownership interest in the corporation.

An advantage to trading stocks is that it's one of the most basic forms of trading the markets. You don't need any kind of special broker account to get started, and you can begin with a relatively small account. The main disadvantage of trading stocks is that you have no leverage with your money, meaning that it takes a dollar to control a dollar's worth of any given stock.

ETFs – An Exchange-Traded Fund (ETF) is a fund that trades indexes or specific sectors. ETF trading is one of the more popular forms of trading. Some of the most common forms of these indexes are the S&P500, the Dow Jones Industrial Average, and the NASDAQ Composite. Some of the most common sectors include bonds, metals, commodities, technology, and healthcare. ETFs are similar to mutual funds as they are made up of a portfolio of stocks. However, unlike mutual funds, they are actively traded during normal market hours in the same manner as stocks.

ETFs are priced and traded continuously throughout the trading day; therefore, they hold a significant advantage in the flexibility that they offer over mutual funds. When trading ETFs you can buy them, sell them short, hold them as long-term investments or trade them regularly as you would trade individual stocks.

With ETFs can take advantage of the diversification that goes with investing in entire markets, sectors, regions, or asset types. Because they represent groupings of stocks, the more actively traded ETFs (especially those based on major indexes), will typically trade at much higher volumes than individual stocks. Higher trading volume means higher liquidity, which enables you to get into and out of investment positions relatively easily and with minimal expense. ETFs incur much lower management fees than do mutual funds.

One approach I recommend to my students trading ETFs is to allocate a different mix of their portfolio to different types of ETFs, depending on their risk tolerance. The following table illustrates a typical mix for an aggressive, moderate, and conservative ETF trader.

	Aggressive	Moderate	Conservative
Equity Index & Large Cap, Financials, Real Estate, Basic Materials	15%	15%	10%
Equity Mid & Small Cap	20%	10%	10%
Emerging / International Markets	35%	25%	20%
Bonds	10%	40%	60%
Precious Metals, Currencies, Energy	20%	10%	0%

Figure 13 - ETF allocation based on risk tolerance

Options – Stock options are contracts that give the buyer the right but not the obligation to buy or sell an underlying stock at a specified strike price on or before a specified date. The seller incurs a corresponding obligation to fulfill the transaction, which means that they must buy or sell the underlying stock if the owner elects to exercise the option, prior to the options expiration date. The buyer pays a premium to the seller for this right. Options which give the buyer the right to buy a stock at a given price are called "calls" and options which give the buyer the right to sell a stock at a given price are called "puts". Both calls and puts are commonly traded.

Options are typically thought of as a higher risk type of investment that only very sophisticated traders should consider using; however, this is not necessarily the case. To trade options you need to open what's called a "margin account" with a broker. And while it is true that you must be a little more financially able to open up such an account (usually a $5,000 minimum), there are many options strategies that are very low risk. Some are simple, some are relatively complex, and some options strategies are used to provide income on an ongoing basis. Options provide very high leverage and as long as you do not abuse that leverage, trading options properly can be less risky than trading the underlying securities directly.

Mutual Funds – Mutual funds are sponsored by holding companies which pool investor dollars together and use the money to purchase large blocks of securities in particular types of investments such as stocks, bonds, cash instruments or municipal securities providing capital growth or cash flow to the investors. One of the purposes of a mutual fund is to give the average investor the opportunity to participate in the equity and debt markets while giving them a place to park money for the long term while hopefully adding to it over time and achieving a decent positive rate return. Mutual funds do, however, incur much larger management fees than do ETFs.

A mutual fund will provide far more diversification than most individual investors could achieve on their own. The thinking of course is that a buy & hold strategy will work over a long period of time because growth mutual funds are invested in the stock market which, of course, has always been believed to go up over a long period of time. But because of the stresses in today's financial markets, this is no longer the case.

Mutual funds are a very common type of investment whose concept has permeated many facets of our investing world in one way or another. Individuals can purchase mutual funds directly or through a financial planner, a stockbroker, some insurance agents and even some banks. They can be used for regular investment accounts or retirement accounts such as the various types of IRAs that can be used. Most 401(k) plans or other company sponsored retirement plans use mutual funds as the selections that are offered to the plan participants as their investment choices.

Forex – The foreign exchange market, or forex for short, is a market where you can trade currencies from various countries, such as the US Dollar, the Euro Dollar, the Japanese Yen, and more. It's the largest financial exchange in the world, and can trade upwards of trillions of dollars each day. This is well above all the volume in the U.S. markets combined.

There are many advantages to trading the forex market including the fact that it is open 24 hours a day. To give you a visual representation of this, here's a figure showing the hours various regions of the world are open for trading.

FOREX MARKETS																							
AM												PM											
1	2	3	4	5	6	7	8	9	10	11	12	1	2	3	4	5	6	7	8	9	10	11	12
		LONDON																					
				NEW YORK																			
								SYDNEY															
								TOKYO															

Figure 14 - Forex trading sessions around the world

In this figure you can see an overlap between the London session and the New York session, between 8am and 11am EST. The currency markets experience the highest volatility and volume during that overlap, which also coincides with the releases of important US economic releases.

The forex market is also a highly liquid market, and it has a high amount of leverage that allows you to control a lot of money with a small amount of capital. Brokers usually do not charge a commission for your trades; you just pay the spread (the difference between the bid and the ask price) for the currency pair you are trading. The forex market allows you to do the same types of trading you would do in most other markets. For example, you can buy long and sell short, you can use stop losses, and you can set profit targets.

When trading currencies they are traded as "pairs". This means that you are not trading just the US Dollar or the Euro Dollar individually. You will trade them together such as the EUR/USD, which is the Euro Dollar/US Dollar currency pair. The relationship in value between the two currencies will determine their exchange rate and whether the pair goes up in value or down in value.

So, that's just a broad overview of the major kinds of trading vehicles you have at your disposal. Some people exclusively trade one or the other, while others trade a mix.

But whatever you choose to do, the strategies and ideas I present in this book apply to all of these different trading vehicles. Later on, as you get into the specifics of a particular trading program you'll learn about strategies and techniques that are unique to the underlying vehicle you are trading.

To get access to my archive of trading articles that will help you trade stocks, ETFs, options, mutual funds, forex, and more, go to **www.BuildWealthBonus.com**.

Chapter 6

Trading Time Frames

There is seemingly no end to the number of different market time frames that traders can choose from such as long-term (years), intermediate-term (months), short-term (weeks), very short-term (days), and day trading (hours or minutes).

Successful traders have emerged in all time frames. Some focus on the long-term only, others on day trading, and still others on all combinations between these two extremes. The point is that you have the potential to build wealth in any of these time frames. The key is to select the time frame that is best suited to your personality and situation. Of course, you will need a good trading methodology that applies to your time frame.

Let's take a look at the different types of time frames most commonly used by traders.

Scalping	Day Trading	Swing Trading	Position Trading	Investing
- Minutes	- Minutes, Hours	- Days, Weeks	- Weeks, Months	- Months, Years

Scalping – This style centers around taking profits on small price changes, typically right after a trade has been entered and has become profitable. To be successful in this style, you need to have a strict exit strategy because one large loss could wipe out the small gains that have been obtained. Having the right tools, such as a live data feed, a direct-access broker, and the time to place many trades is required for this strategy to be successful.

Scalping achieves results by increasing the number of winners and sacrificing the size of the wins. This style is all about quantity over quality.

Day Trading – Day traders are in and out of a position during the trading day. Entry occurs at or on the open of the day and exit occurs before or on the close of the day. Day traders are looking for big one day moves in the market that provide sufficient profit opportunity relative to the risk of being in the market for just a few hours.

Next to scalping, day trading is the most demanding form of trading, as you have to react on a second by second basis in order to take advantage of abrupt moves in the market and at the same time protect your account from unreasonable risk.

Swing Trading – This type of trading is very popular for many at-home traders. By using technical analysis to look for stocks with short-term price momentum, a swing trader will look to capture gains in a stock within a few days to a week or two at the most. Generally speaking, a swing trader is only interested in a market's price trends and patterns.

When using swing trading you must act very quickly to capture the maximum profit potential in a relatively short time frame. Larger trading firms use larger size trades, and therefore do not use this method. Therefore, individual traders are able to exploit such short-term stock movements without having to compete with the major traders. Unlike day trading, swing trading does not require you to monitor the markets during market hours and is therefore far less stressful. All analysis and order entry and trade management can be done at your leisure after the market closes for the day and before it opens the following day.

Position Trading – This is entering into trades with a much longer trading horizon than is the case for swing trading. This style of trader is one who holds a position for a much longer period of time (weeks or months). These long-term traders do not worry about small fluctuations, as they believe their long-term investment will pay out in the long run.

Investing – On the far end of the time frame spectrum is investing. This type of trader typically holds positions for months or years and is, in general, someone who still believes in buy & hold.

I've found that the "sweet spot" time frame that gives you the best return for the actual time you spend managing trades is either swing trading or position trading. Definitely some form of "end of day" trading, where you only need to place and adjust your trades after the markets close, usually in 10 minutes or less at a time.

However, I do have students who are solely day traders who have the potential to do quite well in the markets, as well. The only time frame that I advise my students to truly avoid at all costs is the "investing" time frame of months or years.

Don't forget to access your free bonus training materials at **www.BuildWealthBonus.com**.

Chapter 7

Why Most People Lose

It's a well-known fact that at least 90% of people who trade the markets end up net losers. It could be even higher than that.

Fortunately, it's very easy to correct the primary reasons people lose, so let's take a look at what those are.

1. People lose because they don't have a good trading method.

This is the number one reason for all the big losses most people suffer in the markets. They lack a good trading method. This is a step-by-step process that is easy to follow and that's based on good, proven trading principles.

A good method manages risk first by getting you out of a bad trade as quickly as possible, and it also keeps you in a winning trade for long as possible in order capture the most profit potential.

If you don't have a good trading method, this is what you will typically experience.

First, you have a series of small losing trades, one after another, followed by a small winning trade.

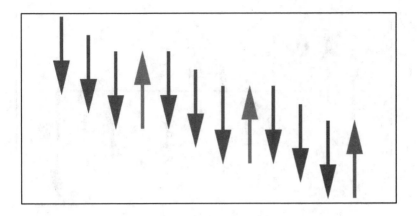

Figure 15 - Small losing trades followed by a small winning trade

Then this pattern repeats - a series of small losers, followed by a small winner. The net result, of course, is that your account gets smaller and smaller until it ends up getting wiped out.

If this is happening to you, then the main problem is that you're not letting the winning trades run.

And here's the other scenario.

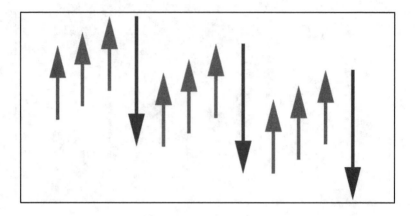

Figure 16 - Small winning trades followed by a big losing trade

You have a series of small winners followed by a big loser that wipes out all the gains you just made. And, again, this pattern repeats itself - small winners followed by a big loser. But just like the first scenario, the end result is the same - you wipe out your trading account.

If this is happening to you, then the main problem is that you're not cutting your losses and getting out of the losing trades fast enough.

You want to manage risk first, and then go for profits. Most people try to grab profits first and risk management is an afterthought, or a reaction to what's happening in a trade.

But when you have a repeatable plan to manage risk first, you know the maximum amount of money you can lose before you even place a trade, and that's a powerful situation to be in because it gives you the peace of mind you need to let the trade run to maximize its profit potential.

This is a really big deal, but unfortunately it's not something that most people think about

2. People lose because they become impatient and force trades.

Most people feel like they have to be trading *all the time*. They need "action" to feel like they're doing something.

A good trading method will keep you out of the market when it's too dangerous to trade, and when the odds are against your success. But most people feel like they're missing out on something if they're not in the market. This is when they'll force a trade by ignoring their method and just going for it.

The sheer act of trading itself becomes more important than the end result, and, as you might expect, this usually only leads to disaster.

Here's a little secret that all successful traders know: *Knowing when not to trade* is equally important as knowing when to trade. While many people suffered huge, account-crippling losses during the 2008 market crash (some even losing 50% or more of their life savings), you might be surprised to hear that the most successful traders weren't sweating the crash at all – that's because they saw the signs that kept them out of the market entirely – all in cash – so that they didn't suffer any major losses. They just waited patiently until a good opportunity presented itself where the odds were in their favor before placing a trade again.

3. People lose because they let their emotions become the basis of their trading decisions.

The primary emotional drivers of fear and greed are the main culprits that get traders into trouble. Fear that you're going to miss out on a good trade or fear that the losing trade you're in isn't going to recover, for example. Or, greed kicks in and keeps you in a trade that you should've exited long ago because you think there's more money to be made. Greed is also responsible for forced trades, or over-trading.

It's easy to get caught up in the excitement of trading, and it's easy to throw discipline out the window in the heat of the moment. That's why practice or demo accounts are a good thing to use when you're trying out a new trading method. And that's why it's good to only trade with money you can afford to lose. Otherwise, you will place unnecessary "have to win or else" pressure on yourself.

Trading discipline is indeed difficult to master, but all successful traders strive toward improving this on a daily basis.

4. People lose because they "go with the crowd".

Whenever I find myself in a discussion with a stranger and they found out about my business, inevitably they'll ask me, "Got any hot tips? What stock should I buy?"

Questions like this immediately tell me that these people have no business trading. They're just "going with the crowd". They tend to use phrases like "playing the market". They're big fans of the bombastic Cable TV talking head personalities that prance around the screen and make wild predictions about the next hot stock to buy.

This is all about pure entertainment and not about having the potential to build wealth. There's nothing wrong with talking about "hot tips" and following a famous "guru" if you're just doing so for entertainment. But if you actually put any real money on advice from this kind of activity, do not be surprised if you lose it all.

Successful traders know this is all nonsense, and so they avoid it at all costs. Remember that the crowd, including the analysts, is most bullish at the top and most bearish at the bottom.

5. People lose because they have unrealistic expectations.

What kind of yearly return do you think is good? Is 30% good, or is that too low? 100% certainly sounds better. Why not an amazing 300% per year return? Wow.

Of course, anything is possible. Yes, you could triple your money. You could also win the lottery. But the reality is that you won't do either of these things.

Unfortunately, there are many unscrupulous firms that continue to make promises like that. And even though you probably know that their promises aren't realistic, your expectation artificially rises in your mind as to what *is* possible.

Another unrealistic expectation is that it's possible to win every single trade. You'll hear the hucksters proclaim, "No losing trades ever!" Really?

So, the utopia of no losing trades coupled with promises of tripling your money with little or no work on your part have indeed littered the collective conscious of the general public.

But successful traders know, of course, that you *will* have losing trades. Even the best trading methods will not only have three, four, or even five losing trades *in a row* on occasion, they'll also have *entire losing months*. Ask yourself, would it be OK with you if in any 12-month period your trading method had four losing months and eight winning months yielding a net double-digit profit at the end of the year?

But of course, amateurs expect to win every month and can't handle this reality and that's why they easily give up and conclude that whatever trading method they were using doesn't work.

Let me tell you about a phenomenon I see time and time again with beginner traders who come to me for help. They try out one of my premium trading programs – something that thousands of existing regular people from all walks of life have been using for *years*.

Well, the beginner may start using the program when the market is quiet, when there aren't any good trading opportunities. So they'll complain to me and get upset because there aren't any trades to be made.

Or, the beginner will get into some trades right from the get-go, and they'll experience three or four losing trades in a row. Or their first month with the program ends up with a net loss. Again, they complain to me that the program they're using isn't any good because they didn't make money in the first several weeks using it.

But all the while, the thousands of other people who are using *the exact same program* don't complain. That's because they understand that even the best methods will suffer occasional losses.

The other thing that happens with some of my beginning students is right from the start they experience massive gains in just a few weeks and heap praise upon me and my trading methods. But then they set themselves up for failure, expecting massive gains every month, oftentimes overtrading, and throwing discipline to the wind.

If you remember the earlier chapter on having a wealth mindset, you'll remember that the poor tend to think of things in *weeks*. These beginners who give up so easily are clearly only thinking in weeks. And what usually happens is that they spend their time going from method to method, making a quick evaluation based on what happens in just a month or two, and they're never satisfied.

I urge you to not get caught up in that kind of thinking. If you have realistic expectations, you'll have the potential to build wealth *much more quickly*.

Make sure you visit **www.BuildWealthBonus.com**. There are a lot of extra free training bonuses waiting there for you to help you build wealth in the markets.

Chapter 8

What's In A Good Trading Method

What is required in successful trading are good trading methods that point you in the right direction to take advantage of higher-probability, lower-risk trading opportunities that set up in all markets over and over again. This doesn't mean that every trading opportunity will be profitable or that losses will not be taken. But it does mean that with good trading methods you will have an edge when trading the markets that should put the odds in your favor.

So by definition, there will be losing trades; in fact, losing trades are quite common when trading. Just because a trading method puts the odds in your favor does not mean you will not experience losses. And that fact leads to one of the keys to trading success. That is, you must control losses.

The whole idea around trading is to win more than you lose and to stay in the game, so to speak, so you have the opportunity to come out a net winner. If you risk too much on each trade, then you can easily deplete your account size down to a level from which there is no recovery. A series of losses could wipe out your account altogether which, of course, would knock you out of the game with no chance of recovery from the profitable trade potential that followed. So you must control losses first and foremost.

Controlling losses is referred to by different names such as risk management, money management, account risk management, stop loss orders, portfolio risk management, limit position size, and so on. But those terms all refer to the same thing - keeping your losses relatively small in relation to your account size so you have the opportunity to trade over a series of trades that has a positive expected outcome, where any losses are more than covered by the profitable winning trades.

Once you understand how to control losses, you still need good trading methods that will guide you in finding the very best trading opportunities at any given time. A good trading method, using primarily technical analysis, should define fairly objective setup conditions, entry rules, stop loss rules, and exit strategies as well as the scanning criteria necessary to find those trading opportunities that are likely to meet the method's setup conditions.

Here are some general attributes that a good trading method should have. If you're currently trading, ask yourself if the method you're trading exhibits all these properties.

- A good method is one that is fairly easy to understand or else you will not follow the method even if it produces favorable results.

- A good method will use no more than a handful of technical indicators from the over 100 available, but use them in an uncommon way to give you an edge over other traders.

- A good trading method requires some discretion on your part to know when to stand aside even when your method tells you to enter into a trade. A good method will highlight those instances when you should stand aside and not take the trade, but it is still up to you to recognize when these instances occur and take the appropriate action.

- A good trading method should complement other trading methods so that a suite of trading methods work synergistically together in order to mine the maximum profit potential that the markets have to offer. Market price action sets up in different ways in advance of higher probability, lower risk trades and in order to capture these opportunities, ideally a complementary set of trading methods should be available in your "trader's toolbox" to be able to take advantage of these opportunities when they occur.

One method alone would only have the ability to capture some of these opportunities.

- A good trading method, once it is mastered, should require very little time to apply to the markets, usually 10 minutes or less per trading session. After the markets close each day, a good trading method should be the basis for your trading routine each day. The markets close, you update your charting software data feed, and all indicators and price data are updated in seconds. At the same time your charting software automatically helps you find the best opportunities that meet your method's setup conditions. You then review the charts for those markets selected confirming that the setup conditions are in place, determine your entry point and place your orders online in a matter of a few minutes.

- A good method allows you to easily manage your trades once you have entered the market requiring minor adjustments to your trailing stop orders each night.

Now let's take a closer look at each one of the key attributes of a good trading method.

1. Setup Conditions

These are the specific conditions that must be in place in order for a trade to be considered. Ideally, these should be programmable into your charting software's scanning routine. This is necessary in order to automatically apply these conditions by your charting software each night after the markets close when you update your price data.

Setup conditions can be based solely upon price action, patterns, volume or technical indicators or a combination of these. And the setup conditions should also include filters to select only those markets that not only meet the setup conditions but also have a high likelihood of being triggered into a position the following day in accordance with the entry rules.

But there's a sort of macro setup condition that I put before everything else, and that's the concept of a *deliberately trading market.*

As a trader, you're looking for a market that moves up and down in a smooth, even fashion. Why?

Look at the picture of this gentleman with the long curly hair. Do you know who he is?

It's Sir Isaac Newton, and his First Law of Motion states that, "A body in motion tends to stay in motion unless acted upon by an outside force." Now, Newton probably wasn't taking about  trading, but his First Law of Motion is why we look for smooth markets. And if a market has been moving in a particular direction, it tends to keep moving in that direction unless acted upon by an outside force, which will appear as a change in price direction. So take a look at this chart.

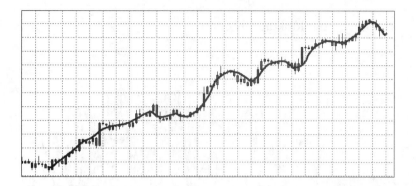

Figure 17 - A deliberately trading market

It doesn't matter what the time frame or the market is. Just look at the smooth movement of the price action. This is a deliberately trading market where one day's price action looks very much like the prior day in terms of the range of the price from the high to the low.

There are no unusually wide-range days here where the price jumps up very, very high and then collapses down very, very low, or closes somewhere in the middle. You don't see any of that on this chart.

You don't see any unusual gaps in price where the market from one day to the next might jump up or might jump down several dollars, creating a gap. You don't see that on this chart. You see a chart where the market is in motion and it's staying in motion, undulating a bit but going steadily up.

Okay, now look at this chart.

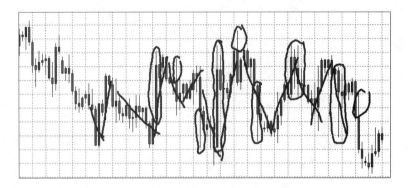

Figure 18 - A non-deliberately trading market

This is an example of a market that is definitely not deliberately trading. You've got several very wide-range days on the price action. You have gaps in prices. You have a helter-skelter kind of price action.

From one day to the next, you don't know if this market is going to go up or go down. You don't know what's going to happen. It looks like an electro-cardiogram where it just bounces back and forth, all around.

This kind of price action spells risk. It is definitely not a market that is in motion and staying in motion. It's a market that's encountering opposite forces all the time, day in and day out. You want to stay out of this kind of market.

56

How To Build Wealth

There's no need to trade this kind of market when you can trade a deliberately trading market. So what most people do when they try to make money in the markets is they just pick or follow someone else's recommendation without regard to understanding deliberately trading markets.

And even if they have a proven trading plan with solid setup conditions, the odds are stacked against them if they attempt to trade non-deliberately trading markets. But if they only trade in markets that are deliberately trading, the odds are overwhelmingly in their favor.

And of course when it comes to trading, there's no such thing as a crystal ball, so the way to build massive potential wealth is to do everything that you can to maximize your odds of success, and that's why a deliberately trading market is such a big deal.

So you can pick any stock and apply this technique to it, and you'll know in an instant whether to stay away or whether to consider trading it. The next time you hear about a stock on television, in the news or from a friend, just pull up the chart and ask yourself: "Is this a deliberately trading market?" You should be able to spot it in seconds.

Just doing that one simple thing will give you a big advantage over all the other people who don't even think to consider that, and that really is a big deal.

This is such a big deal, in fact, that many of my students have told me that this concept is one of the most profound things they've learned from me that has had the biggest impact on their trading results.

Here's an actual quote from one of my long-time students.

"I have used Bill's concept of deliberately-trading markets for some time now to swing trade both stocks and forex.

It cannot be overstated how effective it is.

Do yourself a favor and start practicing analyzing every chart you wish to trade in this manner and see the difference for yourself.

You won't be disappointed."

-Dr. Bruce R.

2. Entry Rules

Once the setup conditions have been applied and a market selected for trading, the method's entry rules must be applied to ensure that the proper order type is used to enter the market.

For example, some methods require price confirmation in the expected direction of the trade before entering the trade. In this case you would use a stop entry order.

But regardless of what the actual entry rules are, there's a simple way to eyeball a market's trend to approximate when you should enter and exit the market.

It's called the "middle one-third" of the trend.

Take a look at this chart where I've zoomed in on a nice uptrend.

Now here's what most people think you have to do to create wealth trading the markets. They think you have to buy at the very bottom of a trend as seen here, and then sell at the very top. Anything less than that is perceived as a failure.

How To Build Wealth

Well, one of the greatest traders of the 20th Century, Bernard Baruch, who was a multi-millionaire and who also went on to become a presidential advisor, had this to say about trying to capture the entire trend. He said:

"Don't try to buy at the bottom and sell at the top. It can't be done, except by liars. I can't help making money. I just wait for the market to bottom. Then I buy on the way up, and then I sell before the top. I'm satisfied with the middle one-third of the move."

Now this is a very, very profound concept, and I want to emphasize this again. Baruch said, *"I just wait for the market to bottom, and buy on the way up. Then I sell before the top.* ***I'm satisfied with the middle one-third of the move."***

That's the secret: the middle one-third. If that doesn't make sense to you, here's another way to look at it. Baseball homerun kings Babe Ruth, Hank Aaron, and Barry Bonds are all masters of the middle one-third. They understood that all you need to do to hit the most homeruns, over time, is to hit the ball one out of every three times you step up to the plate.

What do you think would have happened if Babe Ruth had given up early in his career because he didn't hit the ball 100% of the time? Of course, we wouldn't be talking about him right now.

Just like Bernard Baruch and just like many of the wealthiest traders, all three of these sluggers were satisfied with the middle one-third. So let's look at what Baruch was talking about in a little more detail, so you can implement this concept yourself.

This is the same chart we just saw, but applying Baruch's philosophy to it. This is what the middle one-third looks like. Now, you might be thinking: "Well, what about the rest of the move? I'd be buying too high if I miss the bottom or I'd be selling too low if I miss the top."

Well, that's how amateurs think. They think you need to capture it all, but some of the best traders on the planet, like

Baruch, figured out long ago that the middle one-third of a trend is much easier to take advantage of.

All you need to do is wait for a trend to develop, hop on board, and then sell before it ends. Now, in practice, what you'll actually end up doing is selling a few days after a trend peaks, and that's why the sell arrow points to the spot on the other side of the trend.

It's easy and it's what the rich do every day to keep and grow their wealth.

3. Initial Stop & 4. Exit Strategy Rules

When a new trade is initiated, it is very important to know beforehand how you will exit the trade should it go against your position. Or another way to say that is, don't ever initiate a new trade without first knowing how to exit the position at a loss, should that occur. The initial stop is a key component to controlling and minimizing risk in your trading. The difference between your entry price and your stop loss price represents your planned risk in the trade on a dollars per share basis.

The exact placement of the stop depends on the nature of the setup conditions and entry rules of the trading method that you are using. But in all cases, the initial stop should be set at where you don't expect the market to go, and if it does, you want to be out of the trade because the market did not act as expected and the premise of the trade is over with. You simply get out at that point with a relatively small loss and move on to the next opportunity.

At the same time you need to have a specific exit strategy for taking a profit in the trade.

One of the best ways to manage both your initial stop and your exit strategy rules is to use what I call the *Free Trade Strategy*.

This is probably one of the easiest things you can do to improve your trading results right now. It doesn't really matter what kind of method you use to enter into a position. If you add on the Free Trade Strategy it will undoubtedly minimize your losses and maximize your profit potential.

Now, I'm going to show you exactly how to do this, and once you see how it's done, you'll never look at any kind of trading the same way again. But first, let's talk about poker for a minute.

There's one thing that the world's best poker players and the world's wealthiest traders have in common. Do you know what it is? They both walk away from a hand or a trade as soon as the odds turn against them, and immediately look for another opportunity with better odds.

Kenny Rogers may have said it the best in his hit song *The Gambler* when he sang: "You got to know when to hold 'em, know when to fold 'em."

But the big difference between poker and trading is that in poker you need to actively decide when to fold your hand and take a small loss, but in trading, there's a way to do this automatically. It's called the stop-loss order or just "stop order" for short.

If you're already familiar with stop-loss order, stay with me because I'm going to show you a very powerful way to use it to create what I call a "free trade." It's an exciting concept.

So here's a very simple example. This shows you how a stop-loss order works. Let's say you bought one share of this market for $10 right where the buy arrow is pointing, so now you've got $10 on the line, and you're hoping that the market goes up.

Now what most people think at this point is that their entire $10 is at risk, because what if a catastrophe occurs and the price plummets to one penny? They'd essentially be wiped out. However, you could protect most of your money by simply placing a stop-loss order at the same time you place your entry order.

So let's say all you want to risk is $1 of your $10. What you would do is place a stop-loss order that says: "If the price drops to $9, automatically sell my one share and give me $9."

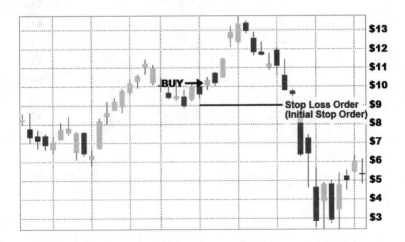

So this line is where your stop-loss order would look like, which is also called the initial stop order. If the price ever hits this line, then a sell order would automatically trigger and you'd get $9 back, losing just $1 or 10% of the purchase price.

Now as you can see in this example, which indeed did happen about 12 days after you paid $10 for your one share, and by the way that's just a 10% loss on this one trade -- not on your entire account.

But what do most people do? They don't use stop orders at all. They just buy and hold, and pray that their investment will go up over time. So look what would have happened in this example if you did not have a stop-loss order.

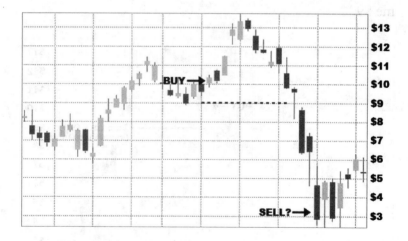

The market crashes hard, all the way below $3 at which point you've now lost $7 or 70% of your investment, if you went ahead and sold at that point. Of course, you could have held onto your position and hoped the market went back up, like it did a little bit here in this example.

But it could have kept dropping even further. The point is, you can't predict what's going to happen so you need to protect yourself.

Well, that's exactly what happened to most of the "buy & hold" investors who thought their money would be safe in the market and were counting on a nice retirement. Their money got wiped out because they didn't have stop-loss orders in place; in fact, they had no exit strategy at all. They weren't willing dump their positions, take a small loss, and move on to a better opportunity.

Now let's take a quick look at exactly what a stop-loss order looks like if you're going to place it online with your broker.

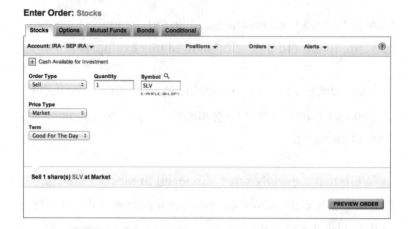

Enter Order: Stocks

Figure 19 - How most people exit their trades (using E*TRADE)

First, this is how most people exit their trades or sell their investments. In this example we're selling one share of an Exchange-Traded Fund called SLV, at a price-type of Market, which means that as soon as you click the sell button, you will sell at the current market price.

This is as simple as it gets, and it offers you no protection, but take a look at the tab on the upper right called Conditional. This is where all the magic happens, but unfortunately most people never click on this tab, which looks like this:

Enter Order: Contingent

Figure 20 - How the wealthy exit their trades (using E*TRADE)

Now, don't be intimidated by any of this. It's very, very simple. This is how you actually place a stop-loss order without tipping your hand to the market makers. Just read through what this says. There are two steps: a condition and an order.

So the condition is if the last price is less than or equal to $9. And the order is sell one share at the market price, which will be right about $9, if this condition is met.

Well, this is how the rich exit their trades, and this is how you place a free trade, which is a very powerful technique you can use again and again to maximize your odds of success in the market. So let's take a look at how it works.

Okay, this is the same chart we were just looking at, but let's clean it up and start from scratch, and approach this market like a trader would look at it. So here's the buy point, indicated by the Buy arrow.

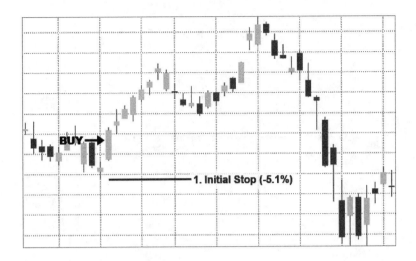

Next, we're going to place the Initial Stop 5.1% below the buy price, which is a typical stop-loss level when entering into a trade. Now here's where the magic starts.

So you can see the initial stop-loss. But as soon as the market moves in favor of the trade by a critical amount, you move the stop from its initial spot all the way up to break even (0.0% gain).

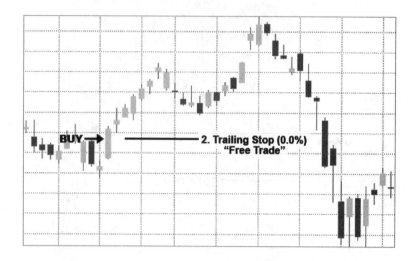

So now your trailing stop is right where you got in, and you've got essentially a "Free Trade". And your initial reward to risk ratio goes from two to one when you put the trade on, to infinity. This means the worst that can happen now is if the market drops back, it gets stopped out at break-even -- a very, very powerful concept -- and if you did get stopped out, you just go onto the next opportunity.

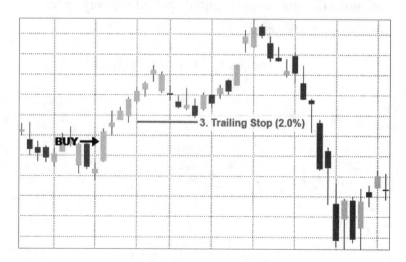

Now as the market continues to move in favor of the trade, you move the stop up from break even to locking in profit below the recent lows. So at this point, we've got the trailing stop locking in 2% profit on the trade.

Depending on price action, you're going to move this stop up more or less quickly. In this case where you have this steady march up making new highs each day, it's usually best to trail the stop below the most recent low.

Next, you're going to move that stop up at the level right below the new lows, locking in now 4.5% profit, and the reason we're trailing the stop, of course, is we don't know how far that market is going to go.

There's no way to know that, so you just keep trailing it up and let it run as far as it wants to go.

And as the market continues to move up, we keep moving the trailing stop up, now locking in now 6.6% profit.

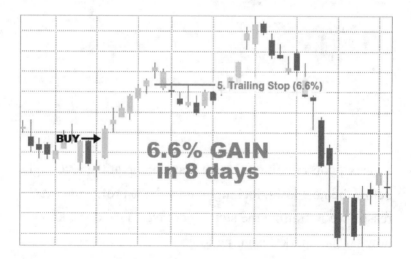

On the bar after we moved the trailing stop to lock in 6.6% profit, you can see the market opened lower, and you'd have been stopped out with a 6.6% gain in 8 days. Not too bad.

Now a lot of traders worry about: "Gee, how do I know if I didn't get out too soon? What if the market keeps going up? Gee, I got out too early," and all those kinds of issues, and that's just a trap for you to lose your discipline in trading.

Because if the market's going to continue to go up, a good method is going to get you right back in, as seen by the new Buy arrow in this chart. So you'd be buying back into the market because it looks like it wants to go even higher.

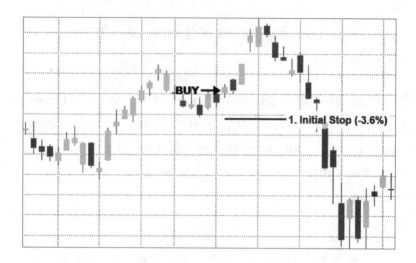

But you don't do that until you get confirmation that it does want to go higher. And again, we place the initial stop just below the recent lows. In this case that's 3.6% below the buy price.

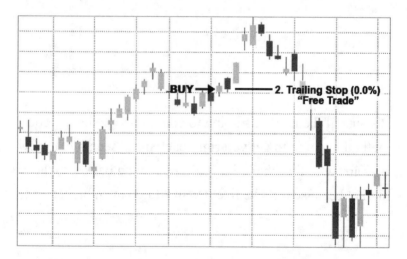

And again, when the market moves up by a critical amount, you would move the stop from the Initial Stop

Level all the way up to break even, giving you a free trade.
The worst that can happen is you break even on the trade.

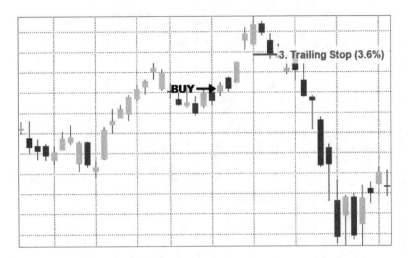

Okay, then with a gap up in price, again, you're going to
want to move that trailing stop up very tightly below, just
below, the low of that bar to lock in profit. Now you're
locking in 3.6%.

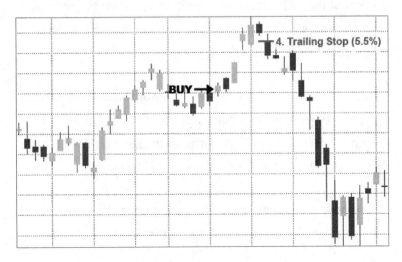

And then we're going to move that stop up even tighter, locking in 5.5% profit.

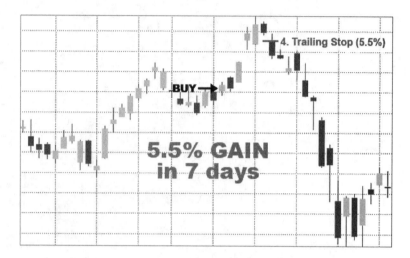

Finally, the market trades lower and you get stopped out for 5.5% gain in seven days.

Now just a side note, a lot of traders are schooled to think that the only trade worth taking is where the reward-to-risk ratio is 3:1 or 4:1. In this case, it was 5.5% gain to 3.6% initial risk. That's about a 1.5:1 ratio.

This 3:1 or 4:1 ratio is a bunch of nonsense. The only way to capture that on a consistent basis is if you win or prepare to win only on 20% of your trades. So don't fall for that myth. That's for the domain of losing traders.

By now you should be getting the picture that the way to build wealth in the markets is to do the opposite of what most people would do. And you should also be getting a sense for how quickly you can place and manage your trades. In practice, after you have learned a good trading method, it really can take less than 10 minutes per day.

For more information on good trading methods, visit **www.BuildWealthBonus.com** for access to more of my best trading tips and techniques.

Chapter 9

Risk Management

It has been said that risk management is more important than the methodology one uses to trade, since an otherwise winning methodology ends up losing without proper risk management, but a mediocre methodology with strong risk management can end up winning.

But here's what most traders do: They get into a trade and focus on how much money they think they can make. Then they worry about risk management after they're already in the trade. That kind of thinking rarely works out.

Successful traders, on the other hand, do the complete opposite. They already know how to manage the risk in a trade before they get into it. Once risk is managed, then they focus on making a profit, all the while continuing to manage risk.

I emphatically agree that risk management is the most important success factor. For example, if you have a winning method that wins on the average 66% of the time, the probability of 3 successive losing trades is 4%. That means you will lose 3 trades in a row 4% of the time for any series of three trades. Further, to illustrate the point, if you risk 33% of your initial capital on each trade you will eventually be wiped out. This is a clear example of a winning methodology undermined by extremely poor risk management.

Much has been written on this subject, its importance, and the means to scientifically calculate the amount that should be risked per trade, but I have found in order for a good trader to consistently apply sound risk management principles, that simpler is better, in accordance with Einstein's adage I told you about earlier.

The technique I strongly recommend to you is to simply risk no more than 2% of your trading account on each trade. By risk I mean the amount you are willing to lose, not the amount applied to make the trade.

For example, with a $50,000 account, you would risk no more than $1,000 per trade. If on the next trade you bought $10,000 of a stock and lost $1,000, your account balance would be $49,000, limiting your risk on the next trade to $980 (2% of $49,000). Unlike the example above, where 3 losing trades wiped out the account, by limiting your risk to 2% per trade, your account would be down only $2,940 to $47,060. On the other hand, as your account grows, you can risk 2% of the growing account balance, which will allow you to grow the account more quickly.

If you're trading a smaller account under $5,000, you can risk up to 5% per trade. That is because the absolute dollar amount of risk on a smaller account is much lower than it would be on a larger account. Also, commission costs begin to be a factor with smaller accounts if your position size is too small which could be the case if risking only 2%. However, never risk more than 5% and only trade with money you can afford to lose. Not that you will lose it, but you don't want the added pressure of having to win.

That said, successful traders with very large accounts will often risk no more than a half percent (0.5%) per trade to further limit risk. This is contrary to what amateurs do when they are fortunate enough to make money in spite of poor practices, only to give it all back by increasing the risk percentage per trade thinking they can do no wrong.

Here's a simple way to visualize this formula. And by following this formula you will always know beforehand the maximum position size (in this case the number of shares) for any one trade.

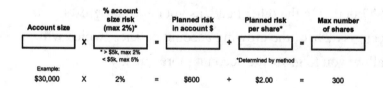

The importance of this simple rule should be self-evident. In order to become wealthy trading the markets, you need to stay in the game and the 2% risk rule will keep you in the game to give your methodology the chance to payoff in the long run.

Remember, if you have a winning trading method, individual trade outcomes are not important, it is the outcome from a series of trades that is important, where you know that the more trades you make the more likely you will be a net winner.

This is, of course, what the casino models are based upon. They don't mind losses up to the house limit, because they know that the odds are in their favor and when the month comes to a close, the casino will be a net winner, time and time again. You want to be like the casino. Work your winning method with sound risk management so that you are not taken out of the game along the way.

Another important aspect of risk management when it comes to trading is to not get caught with several long positions in a bull market reversal or with several short positions in a bear market reversal. The following is a way to hedge for this situation, which will occur sometime in the life of every bull and bear market.

In a bull market, it is always a good idea to have one short position on (only those that would meet the criteria defined in this course) for every three long positions. And likewise, in a bear market, it is always a good idea to have one long position on (only those that would meet the criteria defined in this course) for every three short positions. When the market reverses, often times unexpectedly, you will be able to offset a good portion of the loss from the losing trades with the usually exceptional profit on the one winning trade.

Make sure you visit **www.BuildWealthBonus.com** where you can download a position size worksheet to help you manage risk every time you trade.

Chapter 10

Control Your Emotions

Much has been written on the subject of controlling your emotions when trading in one form or another. This is the psychological, emotional, and discipline aspect of trading. This is the aspect of trading that beginners love to ignore, only to their peril.

WARNING: Do not ignore this chapter, or think it is not as important as the other chapters in this book. The mere fact that you've read this far should be a clear indication that you're committed to improving your trading. Otherwise, why did you open this book in the first place?

For full mastery of disciplined trading, I would encourage you to get a good book or two on this subject, but in this chapter I will give you my thoughts on this important subject.

Your mindset as a trader is about controlling fear and greed. Fear and greed are what drive the markets, and to be a successful trader you must control these two feelings and the resulting emotions that they drive.

Greed can cause the beginning trader to jump in and begin trading before having had the appropriate trading education only to make mistake after mistake with unhappy results. Fear, on the other hand, can cause a would-be beginning trader to never take the first step towards getting educated about trading.

If you understand that trading is a business that is attempting to minimize risk and maximize profit potential, then you know that there will be losing as well as winning trades and that you must get the appropriate trading education to be successful.

It is paramount that when you're winning you do not become elated and flushed with feelings of success. Why? Because the greed factor will likely kick in and then you'll begin to make serious mistakes in your trading – like over-trading, risking too much on each trade, throwing caution to the wind, not using stop orders, and so on. When you're winning, you tend to feel you can do no wrong. Plain and simple, that mindset is a setup for failure.

It is equally paramount that when you're losing you do not become upset and start beating yourself up with a negative mindset. Why? Because the fear factor will likely kick in and then you'll begin to make serious mistakes in your trading – like trying to make up losses all at once on the next trade, by overtrading, taking on far too much risk on one trade, and so on. You may begin to ignore stop loss points and develop such a state of fear that you will not exit a trade that is going against your position to the point of letting that trade's losses continue to grow beyond anything

that was originally intended when the trade was initiated –
to the point of potentially wiping out your entire account.
You can become frozen by fear.

And so the successful trader is aware of this double-
edged sword and maintains a calm, collected, almost
detached attitude regarding both winning and losing trades.

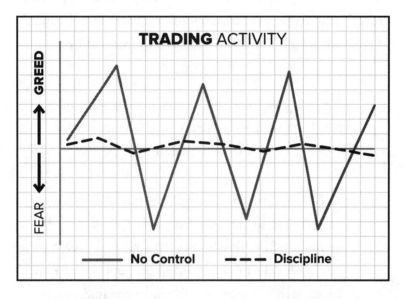

Fear can also prevent a beginning trader or a trader who
has made mistakes in the past with poor results from
pulling the trigger on the next trade. This is especially
common after the trader learns and masters new good
trading methods, but because of the fear factor is afraid to
actually pull the trigger on a new trade.

Greed drives the emotional need to believe in the Holy
Grail of trading or the belief that it is possible to trade

without ever losing, and then when losses do occur such a trader is shocked and dismayed and possibly gives up on trading altogether without ever understanding what happened to them.

So while most traders can understand the pitfalls of fear and greed, the question remains how to control these emotions. And while the answer to this question requires a great deal of understanding and introspection into the mind of the trader, I would like to offer a few practical tips.

1.   I believe that you should never trade with money that you cannot afford to lose. Doing so simply puts too much pressure on you, making it very difficult to control both fear and greed.

2.   Make sure you use the risk management guidelines I covered in the last chapter where you don't risk more than 2% of your account size, and even a smaller level of risk for larger accounts on any one trade. Risking more has the potential to do great damage to your account, not to mention the emotional and psychological damage done. When trading by risking less than 2% of your account size you are much more likely to be able to keep fear and greed in check and remain disciplined in your trading.

3. Master powerful but simple methods to guide your trading. If you have not mastered a good method, then it is safe to say that you have no edge trading the markets and are doing nothing more than gambling. Your trading methods must also be as simple as possible or else you won't follow them. The more complex your trading methods are, the less likely you are going to follow those methods and be able to stay disciplined in your trading. Remember Einstein's advice of "simple is better".

4. Paper trade new methods until you feel you have mastered them, and only then trade with a live account. This allows you to make all of the mistakes that are normal in the learning process with a demo paper trading account that will not rob you of your trading capital.

    Paper trading is an old term that predates computers where you would keep track of trades on paper to see what the results would have been had you actually traded them. Today, many brokers offer a practice or demo account so you can go through the mechanics of trading but only using "play" money. While paper trading is definitely not the same thing emotionally as real trading, it is a good practice to follow.

I believe that by following these practical tips your ability to develop and maintain the right mindset and your ability to keep fear and greed in check is greatly enhanced. These should all be considered a prerequisite to successful trading.

Go to **www.BuildWealthBonus.com** to dive deeper on the subject of trading discipline and mastering your emotions. I have some great bonus reports waiting there for you.

Chapter 11

How To Choose A Trading Program

As I mentioned earlier, I've been teaching thousands of folks just like you how to trade the markets since 2001. Back then there was a ton of trading information online (and offline, for that matter). And today, this information seems to have multiplied exponentially. So where do you begin? Well, trading is a very personal business and I've always maintained that you need to trade with a method that fits your emotions, trading style, and personal lifestyle.

But what are we all really trying to achieve? Honestly. It's not a digital trading account padded with a bunch of zeros, is it? Sure, we all want to build wealth, but what we ultimately want is what that money can do for us.

There's something to be said about lifestyle, and you need to ask yourself a very personal question. What's the right mix of trading and non-trading activity for you? When it comes to balancing this, I think I've been through it all. In my early days, when I was killing myself to capture profits day trading, my life outside trading suffered and took some big bruises. I remember at least a few times where I would be in a very critical meeting at my day job, where my focus was needed 100% to truly be effective, but my mind would wander to that open trade I had just placed an hour earlier. So not only did my effectiveness at work suffer, but my trading did, too.

And there was also a stretch of time when I'd get home from a long day of work, see my wife and kids at dinner and then disappear into my trading "lair" with a pot of black coffee, as my wife put the kids to bed and fell asleep without me.

Here's an actual photo that my son, Greg, took of me around 1980 while I was deep in analysis.

Figure 21 - Analyzing charts circa 1980

These are some of the events that drove me to discover trading methods that only required 10 minutes or less per night to apply. And when I began sharing them with the world in 2001, I found out I was not alone. There were thousands of traders out there who felt just like me.

However, that's just my experience, and my story. You need to look at your story and decide what's right for you. Everybody is different.

So to help you evaluate a trading program, here are some questions you should consider.

1. Was the trading program developed by someone who actually trades?

It's important that any trading program you are considering was developed by someone who actually trades the markets, and not just someone who read a few books and cobbled together something that looks good on paper.

Theory is one thing, but practice is something entirely different. Real traders know this, and any good trading program will have caveats or exceptions to the rules based on real world experience.

2. Does the developer of the trading program have years of experience?

When you invest in a trading program you're paying for someone else's experience. You're leveraging all the time they already spent testing ideas, and all the money they already traded in the markets to see what actually works.

An experienced trader is also usually immune to the latest fads and can see through the usual hype. They have control of their emotions, they've been through several market crashes and survived to tell their story, and they've probably experienced every emotion you'll experience.

That's the kind of person you want to have your back.

3. Does the trading program provide ongoing support?

When you select a trading program, you *will* have questions, no matter how good it is. It's only natural. That's why it's imperative that a professional team is in place to help answer your questions.

When it comes to trading, I've found that email support is one of the best ways to resolve questions. It allows you send images of the trades you have questions about, and it provides a convenient thread of your conversation that you can refer back to.

If you're able to find live support in the form of webinars (web-based seminars), that's an added bonus. In this format, the program developer can share his or her computer screen which you see live on your screen. Then you can interact with them while you're both looking at the same chart. It almost feels like you're sitting next to each other, and it's a great way to learn.

4. Does the trading program match your temperament and schedule?

Because trading is so personal, the trading program you choose needs to match your temperament. It also needs to match your schedule.

The world's greatest day trading program that requires you to watch the markets all day will no doubt be a failure in your hands if you can only trade in the evenings.

So, make sure you have a good understanding of the practical day-to-day mechanics involved in trading with the program that you choose.

5. Does the trading program have specific, step-by-step rules?

Trading programs based on arbitrary decisions, on hunches, or on emotion probably will not give you the kind of results you're looking for in the markets.

The key to building wealth long term in the markets is to have a set of emotionless rules you can follow day in and day out that take care of as many variables as possible for you. There should be step-by-step rules so that you know exactly what to do, no matter what happens in the markets.

6. Is the trading program simple to apply?

Amateur and beginner traders mistakenly think that the more complicated a trading program is, the more effective it is. They become enamored with technical indicators and think, *the more the better*. Nothing could be further from the truth, and in fact, the opposite tends to be true.

If a trading program is too complicated and too onerous to implement, you will either never use it or you will use it incorrectly.

Instead, you need a program that's simple enough where you can apply it without too much work, but also unique and uncommon in how it analyzes the markets, thus giving you an edge over other traders.

7. Is the trading program aimed at liquid markets?

It's critical that whatever trading program you choose can be applied to liquid markets, or markets that have sufficient daily volume to easily and consistently execute orders as intended.

If you refer back to the discussion on deliberately trading markets, that kind of a market tends to be a liquid market, and a non-deliberately trading market tends to not have as much liquidity.

Good trading programs should include some sort of mechanism in their selection criteria that filters out the low-volume markets.

8. Will the trading program work in both bull and bear markets?

A good trading program should be dependent on just a bull market for its success. It should have the potential to generate successful trading performance in all market conditions: bull, bear, and sideways.

Sometimes, beginner traders are afraid to "sell short" in a bear market because they've heard that selling short is risky. Well, selling short is indeed risky if you don't know what you're doing.

However, what is even more risky is owning stocks that are plummeting, not to mention missing out on all the profit potential that exists in bear markets. Experienced traders can tell you that you can often make more money in a bear market because it tends to drop more quickly than a bull market rises.

So, make sure you take advantage of all market conditions with the trading program you choose.

9. Does the trading program offer a money back guarantee?

No matter how good a trading program looks on paper, the only way to know if it's going to work for you is to try it out and put it to the test. That's why it's important that there's a money back guarantee. Any reputable firm will offer this.

However, I must caution you again not to fall into the trap that many beginners get caught in. They see a money back guarantee, they invest in a program, and they casually attempt to trade it for a few weeks. As soon as they encounter a losing trade they give up and conclude that the program is no good. In other words, they want immediate gratification with as little work as possible.

Remember that just because you encounter a month with a net loss does not mean that the trading program is invalid or doesn't work. You really need to give it several months or more to get a good feel for it.

Also, beginners tend to implement trading programs incorrectly. They'll misinterpret the trading rules, enter their orders the wrong way, or even override the rules because they think they know something better. And then they conclude the program is no good.

So, use the guarantee period to implement the program correctly before you attempt to alter the rules yourself. That's something that should only be done by very advanced traders.

To download a checklist version of these questions that you can print out when evaluating a trading program, go to **www.BuildWealthBonus.com**.

Chapter 12

Top Trading Myths

Over the years I think I've heard just about every myth out there about trading. Unfortunately, most people take these myths as *fact* without checking to see if they're actually true. Here are some of my favorites.

Myth: Buy and hold is safe because historically the market goes up about 10% per year.

Fact: At one time, an argument could be made that buy and hold was a somewhat safe, if not mediocre, investing strategy. But as you saw earlier, this strategy pretty much stopped working somewhere around 2001.

It's far safer to trade in and out of the many short-term up and down trends that present themselves again and again. Further, there's much more profit potential for you to tap into trading these trends.

And maybe most importantly, one of the biggest dangers of the buy and hold strategy is that you are exposed to untold risk in the event that a big market crash occurs, like it did in 2008. And rest assured, the market will crash multiple more times in your lifetime. That is something you can definitely count on.

So unless you're OK with watching your portfolio take a 50% hit, you should stop using a buy and hold strategy immediately and instead start trading.

Myth: Trading is complicated.

Fact: Trading *can* be complicated, but only if you make it that way. I think this myth stems from the fact that beginners tend to over-complicate things *and* so-called experts needless over-complicate things just to show off how much they know.

Also, complicated trading methods seldom are successful, even if they look good on paper and are supported by lots of analysis and data. Why? Because if a trading method is too complicated, you simply will not follow it properly. You'll start to take short cuts. You'll make mistakes. And ultimately, you're trading a completely different method that doesn't work.

By contrast, I've found that the simpler a method is, the easier it is to apply, and ultimately the better results it will produce.

Myth: You need to buy the bottoms and sell the tops to win.

Fact: The only way you can buy the bottoms and sell the tops in the market is through sheer luck. It can happen, but it won't happen often. This is because there's no way to predict the future price action of any market.

But the good news is that you don't have to buy the absolute bottoms and sell the absolute tops. Instead, all you really need to do in order to have the potential to be very successful is to capture the middle one-third of any given market move.

Remember what Bernard Baruch said: *"I just wait for the market to bottom, and buy on the way up. Then I sell before the top.* ***I'm satisfied with the middle one-third of the move.****"*

Myth: You should only trade in a strong economy.

Fact: For a buy and hold investor, a strong economy is probably something very desirable, and very necessary. However, for a trader, the state of the economy doesn't really matter.

And in fact, traders can often make even more money during times of great economic and political turmoil. Why? Because traders need volatility, or price movement to make the most money. And a quiet, stable economy doesn't create nearly as much market movement, either up or down, as a shaky economy does.

Don't forget, as a trader you don't care if the markets go up or down. With a good trading method, you're just waiting for the right opportunity to go long or to sell short, depending on what the market does. Either way, you have step-by-step rules that tell you exactly what to do and that protect your portfolio every step of the way.

Myth: You must win on every trade.

Fact: This is more amateur nonsense, of course. You absolutely do not need to win on every trade to have the potential to build wealth in the markets, and, of course, such a scenario is neither possible nor necessary.

The key is to know how to manage risk. With good risk management, you can still come out a net winner even if you only win half of the trades you place.

The casino model is the classic example of why you don't need to win every trade. The casino pays out money all the time, but at the end of the day, it always wins because it has an edge. As a trader, you want to be like the casino.

Myth: Automated trading systems will make you rich.

Fact: When searching for a trading program, it's human nature to want to believe that there's some sort of system that can automatically place trades for you and make you a pile of money in the process.

In fact, marketing hucksters prey on this and it seems like every week there's a new automated trading system that *can't lose*! Think about this for a second.

If a system like this actually existed, don't you think all the big companies with billions of dollars at their disposal would be using it? And do you really think it would be for sale for under a hundred dollars?

Everybody wants the "magic bullet", or the Holy Grail. Nobody wants to do the work. That's a fantasy that will get you nowhere fast.

The reality is that automated trading systems aren't necessary to have the potential to build a lifetime of wealth in the markets. How do I know this? Because plenty of traders are doing just that, without the help of junky "get rich quick" gimmicks.

Myth: Short selling is dangerous.

Fact: This myth stems from the fact that theoretically there is no limit to how high a stock can trade while that same stock can only trade down to zero. So, a short position could suffer unlimited losses while long position losses are limited on the downside.

The truth is, selling short is no more risky than buying long as long as prudent stop loss orders are used. In fact, being long in a bear market is far more risky than being short. And of course, being short in a bull market is equally risky. So the riskiness of a position is dependent on the use of good money management methods, not whether you are short or long.

Myth: You must be an insider to make money in the markets.

Fact: Ethical insiders in corporate America are notoriously poor investors in their own company's stock. They do not have an edge on the market. In fact, they are constrained by the SEC as to when and how much they can buy and sell, and you are not.

Myth: With technical analysis, the more indicators the better.

Fact: When a new trader gets their hands on trading software for the first time, it's very tempting to want to plot as many technical indicators as possible on the charts. They look for patterns found by using multiple indicators and summarize that more indicators will give them more insight into the price movement of a market.

The reality is that most traders are using technical indicators in the textbook manner in which they were designed to be used. But if everyone is using the same indicators in the same way, then none of them have an edge. Instead, the key is to use a *few* technical indicators in an *uncommon* way. That's how you get an edge over other traders.

Myth: Market analysts are usually right.

Fact: Like it or not, we live in a society obsessed with entertainment. People love to watch the market analysts on cable TV with big personalities make predictions. They love to hear the stories they tell to justify their stock picks. It's all about entertainment.

The only reason these analysts have a job is because the general public at large thinks they know something about the future of the market. And the reality is that nobody knows anything about the future of any market. They never have, and they never will.

You can't predict what will happen tomorrow. Anything can happen. So, market analysts are usually *not* right. But that doesn't keep them from enjoying very profitable careers as financial entertainers.

Remember to visit **www.BuildWealthBonus.com** for access to more free trading tips, techniques, articles, and reports.

Chapter 13

Why Do You Really Want To Trade?

As you're digesting all the information in this book, I'd encourage you to think about the underlying, core reasons why you're actually interested in trading the markets. For most people, it's because they want to improve or change some aspect of their life that they're not 100% happy with.

So, to help you out, please take a few minutes and complete this short activity. I think you'll find that it will help you clarify where you are, where you want to go, and what it's going to take to get there.

But I have some good news and bad news. The bad news is that the odds are strongly against you completing this short activity. Why? Because most people think they just need the *hard stuff* when it comes to trading – they just want the trading rules. They just want to know which stock to trade. But they spend no time working on their *mental edge*. However, most people don't succeed in the markets, either. Do you see the correlation? The *soft stuff* is just as important, if not more important, then the *hard stuff*.

And the good news? If you're unlike most people and actually take a few moments to complete this activity, then you'll automatically have an edge over all the traders who refuse to do it. Think about that for a minute.

By the way, if you're an analytical, left-brain person like I am, you might find this activity a little weird or uncomfortable – I know I did! But trust me, it forces you to think about what you really want in life, and the first time I did this activity, it was very profound for me. So if you're feeling a little resistance, go ahead and smash through it and commit to taking the first step to creating the future you want right now by completing this activity.

And if you don't want to write in this book, just visit **www.BuildWealthBonus.com** and download and print out the worksheet there that has these same questions.

1. What is your ultimate dream? This can be anything you want (for example, retiring early, traveling the world, sending your kids to college, starting your own charity, and so on). Describe as if you already have and are currently experiencing it right now (for example, "I retired at age 40 and am currently on a world travel tour with my wife. So far, we've visited Italy, Spain, and Portugal, and have 8 more cities to visit this year.")

_____

_____

_____

_____

2. What does your dream look like? Describe it in as much detail as possible. (Continuing with the example above, "My wife and I are healthy and happy as we effortlessly travel first class from country to country. A private limousine picks us up at each airport we land at whisks us off to the next 5-star hotel.")

_____

_____

_____

_____

3. What does your dream feel like? Again, use as much detail as you can. (For example, "It feels so good to be free and to be close to my family. The stress and strain I used to wake up with when I struggled to make ends meet is now gone. I feel totally relaxed and in control for the first time in my life.")

_____

_____

_____

_____

4. Write down 5 compelling reasons why you MUST transform this dream into reality. (For example, "My kids are getting older, and I MUST spend more free time with them before they grow up and move away.")

1) _____

2) _____

3) _____

4) _____

5) _____

5. Finally, write down 5 things that MUST CHANGE in order for you to achieve your dream. (For example, "I MUST dedicate at least 10 minutes every day to studying successful trading mentors", or "I MUST find a good trading method I can rely on so I can have confidence in placing trades".)

1) _____

2) _____

3) _____

4) _____

5) _____

Now, save your answers and keep them somewhere where they can be reviewed every day. Even though I did this a few years ago, I still keep my answers next to my trading computer. It inspires me to stay focused and on target, and I hope this helps you do the same.

Chapter 14

Pay It Forward

So that's about it for this book, but before I close I want to touch on a very important concept that goes way beyond just "trading".

Now if you only care about money, maybe this won't resonate with you, but for everybody else, listen up.

At this stage of my life I think a lot about family and relationships and people and community. It's easy to get distracted when we're all out there on a daily basis hustling to make more money, but ultimately the money really gives you freedom. Freedom to choose what to do with your time, where to live, who to spend time with, who to help, and so on.

And I really believe that people like us - folks that have an abundance mindset and see money as a good thing -

we're the ones that have the power to help change the economy, and ultimately the world. Now I know that might sound a little lofty, but if you do nothing else than help one family member with the knowledge you learn trading the markets, that can go a long way.

In fact, I think we have a duty to at least try to make a difference. And what's the worst that can happen? You helped somebody out, and that's always a good thing.

So if you know someone who could use a little extra money, share this information with him or her. Get together with a friend or family member and show them what you've learned and how you're using that knowledge.

Just remember the "crab mentality" phenomenon I mentioned in the first chapter. If you encounter a little resistance, give people time and those that are ready and willing to learn will eventually come around.

I truly believe that when the universe at large sees you as a conduit for distributing knowledge and wealth, it will bestow upon you more knowledge and wealth than you will ever need.

Maybe it's silly to think that trading the markets can make a difference in the world, but I know for a fact that it does have the potential to change lives.

It's changed mine and I sincerely hope it can change yours.

Chapter 15

What Now?

Well, if you've read this far then you're probably itching to get started building wealth by trading the markets using the principles you've learned in this book.

The way I see it, you have 2 choices: the slow path, or the fast track.

1. The slow path is to read and study my complimentary training material that my staff of professional traders and I release in various formats. We publish trading articles on our main website, we post technical trading "how to" videos, and we send out bonus reports and other training materials via email to our readers.

2. The fast track is to try out one of my premium trading programs that walks you through every last bit of detail you need to have the potential to build wealth in a variety of markets, including stocks, ETFs, forex, options, and more. Over 40,000 regular people have tried my programs, and many come back to me again and again to keep improving their trading.

How To Build Wealth

I suppose you have a third choice, too, and that's to do nothing. But really, if you've read this far, I know you're not going to just fold up shop and quit. You're not going to give up. There's just too much opportunity out there – too much profit potential. Somebody's going to get it, and it might as well be you.

The one thing we all have in common is that we all have 24 hours in a day. But where we differ is in how we use those 24 hours. There's a great quote attributed to Earl Nightingale about time. He said, *"Never give up on a dream just because of the time it will take to accomplish it. The time will pass anyway."* And so, since the time will indeed pass anyway regardless of how you choose to use it, why not make the most of it?

Let me close with a little story about the slow path versus the fast track.

Years ago my son, Greg, and I were at a business seminar. This was early on when we were struggling to grow Profits Run. We knew all about trading, but the normal "business stuff" was a real challenge. At that seminar was a best-selling author who made an offer to join his "inner circle" program. During his presentation, he talked about the slow path versus the fast track.

He said that we could certainly achieve business success going it alone, but it would take much longer, and we would likely make a lot of costly mistakes along the way. That's the *school of hard knocks*, and it's often a very painful way to go.

But then he said something that I will always remember. He said that instead of wasting a bunch of money making mistakes; why not use that money to *buy a seat at the table*. In other words, pay up front for a mentor who's already made all the mistakes so that you won't have to. That is the fast track.

And that's what we did. We invested in our business and we bought a seat at the table. Greg spent a year traveling the world with this author and a group of about 100 other small business owners, learning the fast track techniques to growing a business.

That was one of the big breakthroughs that helped us grow Profits Run so that not only were we able to help more people via our trading programs, but we were also able to create more jobs. It was a valuable lesson, and that one decision we made to invest upfront in good business education has had a far-reaching impact on tens of thousands of people.

So I encourage you to do the same and invest upfront in one of our premium trading programs. We've created a great success-minded community and I think you'll really enjoy being a part of it.

But remember that ultimately you're in control. Whatever you do must be your decision. No one should force you to do anything. If you're ready to move forward and work with me in a higher capacity, I'm here for you. And if the timing isn't right, that's OK, too. I'll still be here when you're ready.

Either way, thanks for reading *How To Build Wealth*. I hope it has given you a little insight into what's possible by trading the markets in 10 minutes or less per day. And if you have any questions or just want to say "hi", please drop me a line. I'd love to hear how you're doing.

Good Trading,

Bill Poulos

p.s. To learn more about our continuing education and premium trading programs and to claim your bonus training material, visit our special *How To Build Wealth* website at **www.BuildWealthBonus.com**.

Notes

Notes

Notes

Notes

Notes